HERBAL DELIGHTS

Text by Lewis Esson
Illustrations by Nadine Wickenden

CRESCENT BOOKS

This book is intended as a reference only. Do not attempt
to treat any illness without the advice of a
professional. The information presented here is not
to substitute for any treatment prescribed by a physician.

Editorial Direction: Joanna Lorenz
Art Direction: Bobbie Colgate-Stone
Production Control: Susan Brown
Hand Lettering: Leonard Currie

First published in 1991 by Pyramid Books,
an imprint of Reed International Books,
Michelin House, 81 Fulham Road, London SW3 6RB.

© Reed International Books Limited 1991

This 1991 edition published by Crescent Books,
distributed by Outlet Book Company, Inc.,
a Random House Company,
225 Park Avenue South, New York,
New York 10003

Printed and bound in Spain

ISBN 0-517-05259-8

87654321

CONTENTS

INTRODUCTION

HERBS HAVE A MAGIC all of their own: their appearance,
smells and flavours are immensely evocative of country
cottage gardens and kitchens, and grandmother's cooking;
their names are heavy with an irresistible old-world charm
and their acknowledged powers evoke the reassuring
wisdom of simpler times.

In an era of increasing concern about synthetic additives in
foods and cosmetics and the harmful side effects of many
prescribed drugs, it is no surprise that there is a renewed

interest in the powerful properties of common herbs. The source of our oldest medicine and our earliest food enhancers, the subtle powers of herbs are once again being widely appreciated and used to great effect.

Where once there was only parsley, a wide range of fresh herbs is now commonly available on supermarket shelves. Many of the new generation of health food shops stock an astonishingly wide range of dried herbs, and in most towns and cities, for the first time in centuries, there are again specialist herbalists, selling fresh and dried herbs in bulk.

Many people grow their own herbs; they are relatively simple to cultivate so long as the soil is not waterlogged or too heavy in clay. Some herbs even thrive in adverse conditions: lavender and rosemary, for instance, love chalky soil that is high in lime, and the mints and bergamot thrive in very moist soil. Some useful and attractive herbs, such as angelica, chervil, lovage and woodruff, grow well in shady spots; feverfew and thyme work well against walls; and mints, chamomile and pennyroyal are ideal for filling spaces between paving – giving off their wonderful aromas when crushed underfoot! Herbs such as sorrel make excellent ground cover, and the evergreen herbs, like holly, yew and laurel, can keep a garden looking good in winter when used in shrub form or as hedges. Low herbs, such as borage, thyme, sweet violet and feverfew, work well at the fronts of decorative beds and borders.

Quite a number of herbs thrive happily indoors, and keen cooks have great success rearing parsley, basil, tarragon, chives and dill (the summer herbs that are usually the most difficult to obtain commercially) in pots on their kitchen window shelves.

Gather herbs only when perfectly dry, if possible, and take only as much as you need or intend to dry or preserve that day. In general, they are at their best just before they are due to flower. Roots, such as valerian and orris, are at their strongest in the autumn. Try to handle herbs as little as possible, and take only the part of the plant required. Dry herbs in a warm room with a good air circulation, well out of direct sunlight. Place them singly on sheets of newspaper or hang in small bundles. Drying can also be done in an oven at its lowest setting with the door left open.

Store dried herbs in glass jars with well-secured lids or stoppers. Again, keep these in cupboards away from light, which breaks down the natural oils. Herbs also freeze well, and they can be preserved in oils and vinegars.

There is a very elemental pleasure to be had from the use of herbs, particularly if you grow, harvest and use your own. With great ease you can be using them to enliven your cooking, improve your health and beauty, decorate and scent your home, and make delightful gifts for friends and family.

MARSHMALLOW MOISTURIZER

*A lotion to moisturize and soften the skin and to
help soothe minor irritations. If the lotion is kept in
the refrigerator, it will last for up to 5 days.
Place 3 tablespoons of dried marshmallow root or
leaves in a bowl, and cover with a generous cup of
distilled water. Leave to infuse overnight, then
strain into a glass jar with a stopper or screw-top.
Apply to the skin morning and evening after
normal cleansing. Adding the lotion to a little
plain cold cream will make a rich
and creamy moisturizer.*

9

SPRING
TONIC SYRUP

*A stimulating syrup that combats fatigue and
refreshes and renews the system.
Put 2 tablespoons each of freshly chopped nettle,
dandelion and yarrow leaves with a teaspoon of
thyme in a mortar, and pulp with the pestle to
form a smooth paste. Add a generous cup of good
clear honey and blend thoroughly. Store in an
airtight jar and leave in a warm place for at least
a day before use. Take 1 to 2 teaspoonfuls first
thing each morning and last thing at night.*

thyme

yarrow

dandelion

nettle

11

LEMON VERBENA SOAP

This deliciously fresh-scented soap keeps drawers and rooms smelling sweet and makes an ideal gift. Put 2 tablespoons of very finely chopped fresh young lemon verbena leaves in 2 tablespoons of warmed glycerine. Keep in a warm place for an hour or two to infuse. Next, finely grate 12 tablespoons of unscented soap and melt it in the top of a double boiler or in a bowl placed over a pan of simmering water. Off the heat, add to the herbal infusion 1 tablespoon of clear honey and a few drops of natural food colouring, if wished. Pour into glycerine-greased moulds and leave to set.

soap

Verbena

13

Tarragon Vinegar

This makes a delicious vinaigrette or hollandaise sauce; you can also use it in a marinade to give a wonderful flavour to chicken.

Fill a large stoppered or screw-top glass jar or bottle with good white wine vinegar. Add 2 tablespoons of finely chopped fresh tarragon leaves for every 2¹/₂ cups of vinegar. Secure the container, and leave to infuse for about 10 days in a warm place, shaking from time to time. Before use, strain the vinegar through a fine sieve or clean cloth and return to the rinsed-out container, adding a whole sprig of fresh tarragon for decoration.

14

Tarragon

White Wine Vinegar

15

BEDTIME

BERGAMOT MILK

---

*A soothing flavoured milk; an excellent and safe
sedative to be taken as a bedtime drink.
Pour a generous cup of boiling water over 2
teaspoons of dried or 1½ tablespoons of chopped
fresh bergamot leaves. Allow to infuse for 3 to 4
minutes. Strain and drink, sweetened with a little
honey if preferred, while still quite hot.*

honey

bergamot

17

Lady's Mantle
Eye Pads

To soothe and revitalize tired, inflamed,
puffy or watery eyes.
Put 1½ tablespoons each of ground dried lady's
mantle and ground dried fennel in a bowl and
pour in a generous ½ cup of boiling water. Leave
to infuse for about 10 minutes. Strain and use
while still warm: thoroughly soak 2 cotton pads, or
2 or 3 pieces of lint layered together, in the
infusion, and place them on the eyes for at least 10
minutes. Gently dab the eyes with cold water. Keep
the mixture in the refrigerator for up to 4
days, but warm through before re-use.

fennel

lady's mantle

19

MAITRE D'HOTEL BUTTER

A classic herb butter to dress grilled or broiled meat, fish and boiled vegetables.
Take 2 tablespoons of butter per serving and soften with a wooden spoon in a bowl. Finely chop some parsley and shallots, and pound a teaspoon of each per serving of butter in a mortar with a pestle. Mix in with the butter and season with lemon juice and black pepper to taste. Roll the compound butter into a cylinder between 2 sheets of waxed paper and chill. Remove the paper and cut across into discs: place these on top of hot cooked food to decorate and make a delicious sauce.

lemon

butter

parsley

shallots

21

PARSLEY & PRIMROSE SKIN LOTION

A lotion to lighten the skin and help fade freckles.
Leave 2 tablespoons of freshly chopped parsley to
stand in a generous cup of cold water overnight.
Pour a generous cup of boiling water over 2
tablespoons of primrose flowers. Leave to cool and
then strain into a screw-top jar and add the
strained parsley infusion. To use, dab the lotion on
morning and evening, and leave it to dry on the
skin. Keep in the refrigerator.

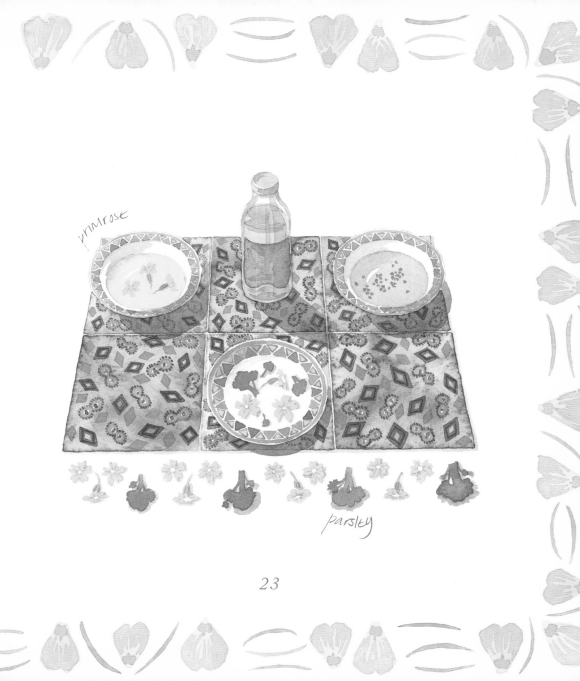

primrose

parsley

23

CHAMOMILE TEA

This relaxing drink induces restful sleep, aids digestion and promotes healthy skin. Tisanes of this sort can be made with many herbs in the same way: for example, bergamot and valerian as a sedative nightcap; mint, borage and salad burnet to refresh and invigorate.

Warm a teapot with a little freshly boiled water. Drain and add 1 teaspoon of finely chopped dried chamomile flowers per person, plus "one more for the pot"! Pour on the re-boiled water and leave to infuse for 3 to 5 minutes – no more. Strain into cups and add honey and lemon juice to taste.

24

lemon

chamomile

honey

25

CLASSIC BOUQUET GARNI

*The classic herb flavouring for all
soups, stocks and stews.
Bind together with fine threads little bundles
consisting of 3 sprigs of parsley, 1 sprig of thyme
and a bay leaf. Either tie them inside a large outer
celery stalk or secure them in a small square of
muslin or cheesecloth drawn up to form a bag.
This makes the bouquet easier to remove before
serving. The basic recipe can be varied for specific
dishes, using other ingredients such as garlic,
rosemary, basil, tarragon, fennel or even citrus
rind, depending on the dish.*

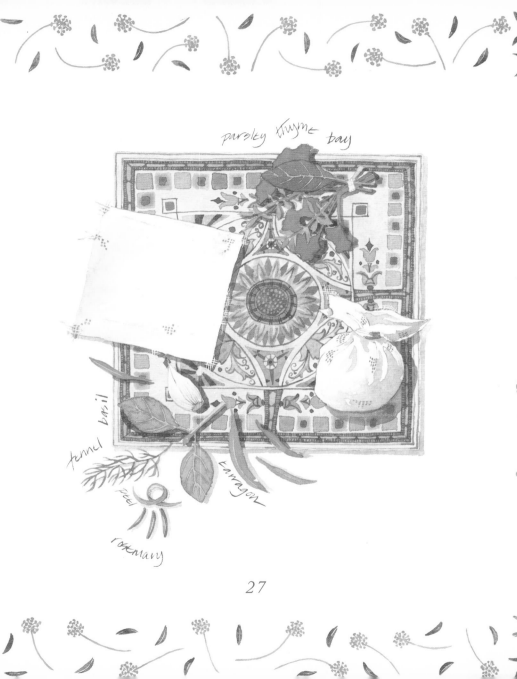

parsley thyme bay

fennel basil

tarragon

peel

rosemary

PEPPERMINT
FACIAL STEAM

Use before going to bed to cleanse the skin, improve circulation and reduce large pores. (Not for very dry skins.)
Boil about 7½ cups of water and pour into a bowl. Add 2 tablespoons each of fresh chopped peppermint and sage and ½ teaspoon of basil. Hold your (freshly cleaned) face about a foot (30 cm) away from the water and cover your head with a large towel. Steam the face and neck for up to 10 minutes. Then, gently pat the skin with a washcloth dipped in iced water and follow up with a soothing face pack.

basil

sage

peppermint

FRAGRANT HERB POT POURRI

In a large decorative china bowl, blend leaves of any or all of the following dried herbs and flowers in equal parts: lemon verbena, lemon balm, sage, basil, rosemary, peppermint, red bergamot, hyssop, sweet cicely, lemon thyme and rose geranium. Add a handful of cloves, 1 or 2 cinnamon sticks broken into lengths, 1 tablespoon of ground orris root and some crushed bay leaves. Next grate 2 or 3 tablespoons of fresh citrus rind and add that. Mix well and top with some dried rosebuds, rose petals, and cornflowers. Add wheat ears and poppy heads for a Harvest Thanksgiving look.

lemon balm

rosebuds

bay

juniper berries

wheat ears

lemon balm

basil

31

WOODRUFF PUNCH

*This stimulating drink is traditionally imbibed on
May Day in Germany. This recipe makes
about 18 glasses.*

*Tie 6 tablespoons of chopped fresh sweet woodruff
and the grated rind of a lemon in a muslin bag.
Place in a large bowl and cover with $1/2$ cup of
Cognac and a half bottle of Rhine or Moselle wine.
Cover and leave to stand overnight. Remove the
bag, add ice cubes, another $1^1/2$ bottles of the wine,
a bottle of champagne and the juice of the lemon
with a little sugar to taste. Serve in long-stemmed
glasses with a fresh strawberry or peach slice
at the bottom.*

strawberry

champagne

peach

woodruff

Juniper Berry Marinade

*To tenderize and flavour venison or to give a
gamey taste to pork or lamb.*

*Gently cook a sliced carrot, onion and celery stick
with 3 crushed garlic cloves, 10 crushed black
peppercorns, 15 crushed juniper berries, a crumbled
bay leaf and a finely chopped sprig of rosemary in
a generous cup of olive oil. When just soft, add a
generous cup of red wine and leave to cool.
Marinate small pieces of meat overnight and large
cuts for up to 10 days in the refrigerator. (Boil
and cool the marinade again after a week!) Use,
strained and reduced, as a delicious sauce base.*

wine

olive oil

vegetables

juniper berries

SAGE & SWEET VIOLET CREAM

Helps alleviate cold sores and soothes and protects swollen, painful or chapped lips.

Put 2 tablespoons each of finely chopped fresh sage and sweet violet leaves, along with 4 tablespoons of almond oil, in a small stoppered jar. Seal and leave in a warm place for about a month, shaking the jar each day. When ready, strain into a bowl and add 4 tablespoons each of almond oil and beeswax which have been melted together. Beat to mix until cold. Store in an airtight jar in a cool place, and apply twice a day or as required.

sage

sweet violet

37

HORSETAIL
INFUSION

*A herbal remedy for strengthening brittle
and splitting finger nails.
In a saucepan, pour 2½ cups of water over 6
tablespoons of dried horsetail stems. Leave to
infuse for about 4 hours and then bring to the boil.
Leave to simmer gently for about 30 minutes,
remove from the heat and leave for another 30
minutes before straining into a stoppered jar or
bottle. Every other day, soak the nails in warm
sunflower oil for 15 minutes and then in a little
warmed horsetail infusion for the same time.*

horsetail

SCENTED HERBAL
BATH SACHET

*This gives a cleansing, soothing and gently
fragrant bath which eases sore joints and muscular
pains and promotes a good night's sleep.
Cut out a piece of muslin or cheesecloth about 9 in
(23 cm) square. In the centre of the square, heap 2
tablespoons each of dried valerian, sage and lovage
leaves. Pull up the corners and tie the sachet
together securely with strong thread. Place the
sachet in the bathtub while running the water, or
arrange to hang it in the stream of water. Sachets
can be re-used, providing they are hung up to dry
after use.*

lovage

valerian

sage

ROSEMARY &
NETTLE SHAMPOO

*A fragrant shampoo that stimulates the scalp,
prevents dandruff and promotes hair growth.
In a small pan, put 2 handfuls of soapwort and
add 1½ cups of water. Bring to the boil and
simmer for 10 minutes. Cover and leave to cool,
then strain into a bottle which has a screw-top or a
secure stopper. Put a handful of young chopped
nettle leaves and 1½ tablespoons of chopped fresh
rosemary in a bowl, and add a cup of boiling water.
Leave to infuse for 20 minutes. Cool and
strain into the bottle. Shake vigorously before
shampooing. Use up within 4 to 5 days.*

43

Aromatic Fennel Oil

Use this fragrant oil to cook fish and seafood, lamb and pork, or in dressings for fish salads. Gently warm enough good olive oil to fill a large stoppered or screw-top glass jar or bottle. Add 4 tablespoons of finely chopped fresh fennel (equal parts white bulb and green leaves) for every 2¹/₂ cups of oil. Pour the oil into the container, secure and leave to infuse in a warm place for about 2 weeks, shaking every 2 to 3 days. Before use, strain the oil and return to the rinsed-out container. Add some sprigs of fennel leaf for visual effect, if you wish.

fennel

45

SCENTED HERB PILLOW

*Soothes and relaxes, promotes restful sleep and
gives a pleasant smell to the bedroom!
Make a pillowcase lining out of linen or hessian
(burlap) and leave open at one end. Make up a
stuffing by mixing dried herbs in the following
proportions: 2 to 3 handfuls each of peppermint,
sage and lemon balm, along with 1 to 2 handfuls
of lavender, dill, lemon thyme, tarragon, woodruff,
red bergamot and rosemary, and 1 to 2
tablespoons of valerian. Fill the pillow loosely with
the herbs, sew closed, and put inside a pretty and
soft pillowcase before use.*

peppermint   tarragon   woodruff

rosemary

valerian

lemon thyme

lemon balm

lavender

sage   red bergamot   dill

47

LOVAGE FOOTBATH

*Soothing, healing and strengthening for
tired and sore feet.*
*Pour 2¹/₂ cups of boiling water on 2 tablespoons of
chopped fresh lovage. Leave to infuse for 15
minutes, then strain the liquid into a foot bath and
top up with hot and cold water to the desired
temperature. Add 1 tablespoon of sea salt and stir
to dissolve. Soak the feet for up to 10 minutes.
Plunge them briefly into cold
water to finish off.*

sea salt

49

CARAWAY COMFITS

Serve after a meal to freshen and sweeten the breath, and to aid digestion.
Dip some large caraway seeds in egg white. Mix a little icing or confectioners' sugar to a paste with some lemon juice. Remove the caraway seeds from the egg, and roll them in the paste. Place them, separated out, on waxed paper and leave them in a cool place to harden.

CARAWAY SEEDS

LEMON

51

ROSEMARY OR CHAMOMILE HAIR RINSE

*Keeps the hair soft and in good condition. It also
stimulates the scalp, removes dandruff and
promotes hair growth.*

*For dark hair, place 2 heaped tablespoons of
chopped fresh rosemary and 1 tablespoon of dried
chamomile flowers in a bowl. If your hair is
blonde, swap the quantities of rosemary and
chamomile! Mix with 2 heaped tablespoons of
dried lime flowers and cover with 3½ cups of
boiling water. Leave to infuse until tepid. Strain
the solution and apply it after all shampoo has
been rinsed from the hair.*

52

lime

rosemary

chamomilk

FRESH
MINT JULEP

*The refreshing and intoxicating drink
of the Old South.
Place 2 or 3 sprigs of fresh mint, or 1 tablespoon
green dried mint, in the bottom of each glass. Add
sugar to taste and just enough water to dissolve the
sugar. Stir the mixture well with a spoon to bruise
the mint and completely dissolve the sugar. Three-
quarters fill the glasses with crushed ice (use a
blender or wrap in a towel and hit with a rolling
pin). Top up with Bourbon (for the authentic
flavour), Rye, Scotch or Cognac. Decorate
with a fresh mint sprig.*

bourbon

mint

55

Parsley Cough Remedy

*Relieves particularly persistent and
stubborn coughs.
Pour 2¹/2 cups of boiling water over 2 tablespoons
of dried agrimony flowers or leaves and 1
tablespoon of dried parsley. Leave to infuse and
cool. Strain into a stoppered jar or bottle. Take 2
or 3 spoonfuls at a time, morning and evening,
and when the cough attacks. The remedy is
especially effective if also used as a
gargle twice a day.*

56

parsley

agrimony

DECORATIVE HERBAL WREATH

*An unusual and aromatic decoration for
door, wall or table.*
*Make a circular frame using wire. Wire sprays of
sweet bay leaves all around to give a base. Tie up
bunches of lavender sprigs with red ribbon and
attach to the wreath with pins. Tie on in the same
way bunches of red rosehips, hawthorn berries and
dried hops. Wreathe in any of the following, either
in sprigs or gathered bunches: lime flowers,
rosemary, lemon verbena, southernwood and
woodruff, chamomile, elderflower and sweet violet.
Finish by studding with dried wild roses.*

lavender

sweet bay

chamomile

hops

wild roses

59

COLTSFOOT &
FENNEL FACE PACK

*Use to soothe, soften and tone the skin, to close
pores and help minimize wrinkles. It's also
effective against acne!*

*Pour ½ cup of boiling water on 2 tablespoons of
dried coltsfoot leaves and 1 tablespoon of dried
fennel leaves. Infuse for 10 minutes and strain.
Blend with a generous ½ cup of yogurt and
enough fine oatmeal to make a thick paste. Wash
the face, finishing with a hot cloth. Cover the eyes
with wet cotton pads, and spread warm paste over
the face. Leave for 10 minutes then wash off with
warm water and a little lemon juice.*

60

lemon

coltsfoot

yoghurt

fennel

oatmeal

ANGELICA MOUTH WASH

A rinse to freshen the mouth and sweeten the breath. Use morning and evening and after meals for maximum effect.

Pour 2¹/2 cups of boiling water over 3 tablespoons of angelica seeds and leave to infuse until cool. Strain into a screw-top jar. You could also add caraway seeds, lemon verbena, peppermint or rosemary to the infusion for extra strength; a little dried orris root will perfume the breath with the scent of violets.

caraway seeds

lemon verbena

peppermint

angelica seeds

rosemary

63

Lewis Esson is a highly experienced author and editor of books and magazines, specializing in food, wine and related subjects. He co-authored, with Jocasta Innes and Arabella Boxer, the worldwide bestseller *The Encyclopedia of Herbs, Spices and Flavourings.*

Nadine Wickenden studied illustration at Brighton Polytechnic in England, graduating in 1986. Besides publishing she has produced work for advertising, packaging and greeting cards.